Wonder Cabinet

Poems by Ryan Mills

RoseDog Books

PITTSBURGH, PENNSYLVANIA 15238

RoseDog Books
585 Alpha Drive
Suite 103
Pittsburgh, PA 15238
Visit our website at www.rosedogbookstore.com

ISBN: 979-8-88729-145-1
eISBN: 979-8-88729-645-6

Wonder Cabinet

*As always, for Courtney and Soren—
The two greatest wonders of my life*

Table of Contents

I.

Dear Courtney 3

Prayers for a Marriage 5

Sharon 8

Ode to a Colostomy Bag 9

Ode to a Fool 12

Drawing with Scissors: Henri Matisse 13

The Last Spectator 15

Table Scraps 17

II.

The Day You Were Born 25

First Laugh 26

Parents 28

Hymn to Hera 30

A House Blessing 32

Junk Totem 35

Still Life with Child 37

An Anything Machine 40

Ear Boy & Finger Cat: Poems for Soren—

    Mysteries of the Ear 45

    Finger Cat 47

    The Impossible Playground 49

Cuckoo Haiku 51
Finger Cat's Invention 55
Finger Cat's Menagerie 57

III.

Wonder Cabinet 61
At the Playground 66
After Pythagoras 68
Driving to the Grocery Store 71
Family Hike: Summer 2020 75
Watching My Son Sleep 79
Dear Soren (Ode to a Geode) 84

I.

Dear Courtney

1

To say I love you is not enough
because you are so much
more than yourself:
a secret river unwinds
within and without you,
never refusing, always carrying
me faithfully downstream.
And I have come upon so many
wonders on my voyage.
I've sailed my boat, my little
boat in which I love you
tenderly along
each generous curve, in and out
of every sheltering
cove until your magic river
spread its dripping wings,
transfigured:
an ocean of pluralities.

Body of water, body of land,
I've known you as a familiar
and as a foreign shore
where elephants of kindness
comfort the weary where
toads bubble up from
the mud of delight.

2

You are a woman who is not
the opposite of a man but rather

the tense and dramatic inter-
play of man and woman,
not only the passive milk-
skinned maiden but also the iron-
browed Lord of the Dead who drives
his rumbling chariot up and through
the earth to seize Kore
by the roots and reap her down
into his bottomless
kingdom. To love you
is therefore to love the whole
world above and below,
and also to see
how your deepest beauty
lies not in the lovely
form you possess
but in what
possesses you.

Prayers for a Marriage

1

Outside our kitchen window,
a hummingbird zig-
zags among the silence

of summer flower trumpets,
its wings so quick-
silver rapid in their beating

that we could be forgiven
for thinking they were frozen
stiff. Not moving at all.

2

May we gather
black sparks.
May we rejoice

as we both are drawn
into the bottomless
difference between us.

3

I remember the ceremony,
the open roof of the church,
the way dark clouds suddenly

poured in overhead, casting

wide nets of hissing rain,
how the guests all rose

in unison as nature's music
drowned out, washed away
Pachelbel's Canon.

4

*Any gift we are able
to consume is not enough. May
we hunger less for our daily*

*bread than for a dense
miracle: a grain of sand
impossible to lift.*

5

All our startled loved ones
fled their orderly rows,
took imperfect and intimate

shelter beneath the gazebo.
You cried laughing as
you were rushed toward me,

hooked into your father's arm.
Among the crowd, a path
opened, let you in. And then

6

the circle closed around us.

O circle closed around us:
each night let us work

ourselves a bit deeper
into the dark
earth of our marriage bed.

7

Outside our open window,
ruby-throated humming-
bird makes no sound at all. Inside,

our busy kitchen reverb-
erates with several competing
songs: garlic sizzle, baby

babble, one of Bach's
cello suites. I clasp
you my wife from behind, kiss

your neck, glance outside.
Our hummingbird is gone.
Or somewhere here in the kitchen?

8

And as our youth
begins to crumble, let us
walk among the ruins,

holding hands
and searching for
God under every stone.

Sharon

is fed by a clear
tube that runs through
a hole in her side.
She cannot taste her food.

She cannot walk upon
her shrunken legs or open
fingers that are forever
locked in twisted & arthritic

knots: unyielding
reminders of the many
things around her
she cannot grasp.

But ask her about
her birthday. Park
her wheelchair out on
the porch so wind

can lift her thinning
hair so sun
can land upon her
upturned face.

She's as much
the queen of this
heartbreaking
world as anyone.

Ode to a Colostomy Bag

O sack of liquid
shit—in difficult
times I recall you
fondly. The dampened
squelching and
squirting and
gurgling sounds that
told me you were
slowly filling;
a heavy ripeness,
almost fruit-like,
tested in the balance
of my hand that
told me you were
full. And then
I would gently
unhook your mouth
from its faithful
grip on Millard's
abdomen, revealing
the tip of his colon—
the stoma—there
where it poked
from his naked
stomach flesh
like the vulnerable
head of a blind
pink worm. In those
days I was only
a few months sober,
my nerves still raw
as Millard's exposed
bowel, my thoughts
often circling

around suicide,
while my spirit
wandered lazily
through an interior
maze of solipsistic
despair. But every
time the time
came to detach you
from my favorite
resident of the Karl
Road Group Home for
Mentally Disabled
Adults, as soon as
I grasped you securely
by the neck,
held you and
your rising sweet-
acidic odors out
to the side and
away from me,
already Millard's
stoma would begin
twitching, gasping
as if for breath,
and suddenly
only one
task mattered:
reaching the toilet,
dumping your hot
smoking contents,
returning to Millard
in time to preserve
a humble portion
of his human
dignity. O friend
of my friend,
every day you
shielded Millard

from his own
corrosive digestive
juices, waste
products and
also from
the embarrassment
of leaking feces
down his pants
and wheelchair. O
instrument of grace,
every day
emptying you
involved me
in rushing back
toward something other
than my own dis-
tress, something simple
but essential,
something bodily
that required me
to kneel, emptied
shitbag in hand,
before the needs
of someone else.
O magic object,
you protected
me from myself.

Ode to a Fool

Who could ever love such an ugly world?
Who would bother to pay
honor to an aging human body as

all day long it grows old and dies?
So many bitter weeds choking, so many
bones stuffing the earth—

it's more pleasant to look up
into the nothing at all
of the sky. Pain quickly disperses

there like a gas. Forget
about the thick, the heavy
mud that sticks to your boots.

It holds no value.
You'd have to be an insect
to treasure all this rotting wood.

You'd have to be a fool
to haul a lumpy brown egg
of rock, a geode,

up from its creek bed, thinking:
"Maybe there are crystal
palaces locked inside."

Drawing with Scissors:
Henri Matisse

white is the saddest color
white like the glare suffusing a hospital
white like the light at the end of the tunnel
white like the sheets on my sickbed
the starched dress of my nurse

white like the blank canvas
to which I can no longer
lift my brushes my wilted
brushes that used to drip globules
clashing dashes of paint

*

drawing close to death means
drawing close to childhood means
learning to draw all over again
this time with a pair of scissors
this time with a pair of assistants

who paint my paper whatsoever
color my heart desires but
this time my heart is simple
happy to let the colors go
as my scissors clip & curve

*

trimming away the excess
slowly liberating green
purple orange fingered fronds
a yellow guitar womanly blue
thighs no longer locked &

lying dormant within the rigid
geometry of construction
paper I wake each morning
renewed as if my life
were only just beginning

*

because I have acknowledged
my life is coming to an end
I am not ridden in my bed
I am riding in a boat
no longer rowing

I stay busy letting go
of paper fruit & paper
hearts & paper stars that flutter
down to cover the waiting
surface of the water

*

all is set afloat

The Last Spectator

He loves the game of basketball
best when the game is over,
the scoreboard blank,

and he's the only soul left
up in the high-rise bleachers.
He loves the private game

that only begins once
the careless crowd has spilled
out into the parking lot,

the game of solemnly observing
what others leave behind:
wadded programs

longing to be scooped
up and smoothed
like crumpled wings,

the lingering tang of hot
breath and sweat and shoes,
trampled popcorn

everywhere. He holds
a single kernel up
to the light of his attention

like a jeweler appraising a diamond.
He touches the empty
seat beside him,

his fingers slowly tracing
the faded grain of the wood
as if he were teasing his way

up an old lover's thigh.
He is achingly alone.
He is anything but lonely,

his friends discarded
candy wrappers, wax-paper cups,
while down on the court

a janitor dry mops
the parquet floor
until it reflects ghosts.

Table Scraps

An essay poem

When I consider the *ontbitjes*—
the "breakfast pieces"—
of the Dutch Golden Age
master, Willem Claeszoon
Heda, I always return
to the same question,
much as Heda persistently
returned to the same
odd little still-life genre:
Why choose to paint the wreckage
left after one's morning
meal is over, the rumpled
tablecloth and half-
empty crystal goblet,
the cast down cutlery,
a tipped over vase,
askew and tilted
plates of partially
eaten food? Why study
the remains rather than
the living breakfast
in progress? Or, why emphasize
the scattered and dis-
heveled, the crumbs, the used
vessels, the done with and
no longer and not
the promise of a table
laid full to bursting, composed
for a feast about to begin?

Poking around on the internet,
or browsing through old Art History

tomes, over the years I've
come across several
well-argued explanations,
one of which places Heda
and other painters of *ontbitjes*
squarely in the *vanitas*
tradition. In nearly all
of Heda's post-breakfast
displays, a half-peeled
lemon, trailing a spiral
of bright yellow rind,
suggests the seductive
appearance, the bitter
taste of mortal life. Sometimes
an open-faced pocket-
watch has been left behind
on the table as if to remind
us: Our brief human life-
time is quickly winding
down. We astute
viewers know that fancy
silver succumbs to tarnish.
We also know a cut-
into, set aside black-
currant pie does not hold
still, that its exposed
inner fruits and juices
soon begin to squirm
with decay. We know the Dutch
term, *stilleven* ("still life"),
is merely a sanitized fiction,
for life is always moving
toward decomposition.
(The Latinate *nature morte*
feels more honest, more forth-
coming in this respect.)

And yet I would object—
Heda's paintings are too lavish,

the play of sunlight on all
those metallic and glass
surfaces too exquisite, the folds
in a crumpled napkin
too precisely, too lovingly
rendered for me to read
his art as a flat and cold
rejection of worldly things.
Are we really to believe
such abundance of sensual
detail amounts to nothing
but a bleak *memento mori*,
that each uniquely broken
bread roll, sleek husk
of cracked nut, cup still
softly aglow with the dregs
of green-or orange or amber-
tinted wine is just another
variation on the same
old religious theme, a stand-in
for a human skull?

Apparently certain critics
agree with my assessment.
They point out that, in particular,
Heda's more ostentatious
still lifes (*pronkstilleven*)
from the 1640s onward mute
traditional *vanitas*
messages and celebrate
the cornucopic wealth
of the Dutch middle class.
Heda's nearly hyper-
realistic portrayal of
polished ewers and
tankards, rummers
(rotund drinking vessels),
their bases studded

with decorative glass
blobs called *prunts*,
imported olives,
crabs shoveled
from the sea in such
overflowing plenty that
to crack one open,
fork out a few buttery
mouthfuls, then leave
the rest of the delicate meat
to rot inside its shell,
probably felt no more
wasteful to a prominent
17th century Dutch
merchant than flushing
one's toilet feels today—
these clear and cleanly
painted signs of prosperity,
of bourgeois affluence
emphasized by the
splendor of its table scraps,
would have made Heda's
work both highly
respected and marketable.
After all, most people,
even stern Northern
European Calvinists,
relish hanging images
of themselves and more
subtly, their implied
successes up on the wall
for themselves and
others to see.

But this socio-economic
interpretation only underscores
the problem with any
anthropocentric

approach to Heda's *ontbitjes*.
As meticulous accounts
of things as they stand
after human beings
have left the room,
I sense that these paintings
hope to lead us
into a realm beyond the human
where food and cloth and
utensil can no longer
be seen as mere possessions,
or even as symbolic
tokens of human mortality.
The meal now over,
there is nothing more for us
to covet or consume and so
a chalky oyster shell,
slurped of its flesh,
suddenly exists
for no one's sake
but its own. A stranger's
food slops curb
our appetite. Their dirty
dishes dampen
our greed for precious
metal. Released
from their status as
objects of human
desire, a licked
silver soup spoon, a cold
and unblinking jelly-
eyed fish confront us with
a sovereignty, an eerie
independence
we cannot easily
dispose of or dismiss
when these abandoned
items, frozen in time

and space, preserved
in paint, are held up
like an inescapable
challenge before our eyes.

Such *Gelassenheit*
("releasement")*
may also explain why
a shattered wine glass often appears
among the array of culinary
debris littering Heda's tables.
Because it is no longer
able to serve as a familiar
tool we grasp in order
to satisfy our thirst,
we are made to see it,
maybe for the first
time as something
strange and wholly
other than ourselves.

*See the writings of Meister Eckhart and also Martin
Heidegger's *Discourse on Thinking*.

II.

The Day You Were Born

As the rumble building up
inside your mother's womb began
spilling out, communicating,

how could anything remain
locked inside itself? Out came the cry:
your mother's yours & mine.

Into my hands fell a slimy blue
umbilical rope hoisting me up & through
the ground beneath my own two feet,

the floor of the delivery room
where I was delivered unto you.
O child raw & steaming, placed

at last on your mother's chest—
the day you were born
you brought me into the world.

First Laugh

You weren't yet
much to write about.
Mostly asleep,

now & then crying,
your fuzzy little
head instinctually

rooting for
Momma's breast.
But suddenly

that day in the bath-
tub, everything
changed as I

dipped & raised
a cup in playful
toast, tipped my wrist

to send a libation
of watery piano
notes tumbling

down into your blue
whale-shaped basin,
down into the frothy

pool from which
each separate drop
first came. O

how your mouth
your eyes your whole
face broke wide

open! & a deep
rumbling chuckle
bubbled up into

your throat. This
was no cry of
necessity, no blind

reaction triggered
by pain or fear
or hunger. Again

& again I filled
I emptied the plastic
cup. Again

& again the sound
of your newly
awakened soul,

testing its freedom
to delight
in nothing at all.

Parents

Swirled tea leaves you pretend to read
at the bottom of my cup. A spider's web
mirage-revolving in the summer
heat like a delicate Ferris wheel.
The child we pass back and forth
between us—an inexhaustible gift.
All these little miracles slowly wear us down.

As early as the middle of the afternoon,
we feel ourselves blurring softly at the edges,
while the air, the light, the everything else
gains contour and solidity, pressing
increasingly upon us in a way
that is somehow both comforting and ominous.
All we can do is lean back

in white plastic lawn chairs and yawn.
Ripples from an unknown source
travel through the shrubbery.
Across the yard, a robin drops off
the chain-link fence, comes in for landing
with the total commitment of a jet plane.
Buhhhrrrd! our little one jump-points.

His confidence and passion
are like a refreshing slap in the face.
At this moment, he's complete smile-
certain that things are always themselves,
that each immature fruit on our apple tree
hangs ripe at hand, labeled, fully present.
He has so many new words to remember,

while we have so many old
worries to forget. Which is why

the burden of having a child lightens us.
We're relieved to know there's someone
among us who's less ambivalent,
more enthused to bear the daily weight
of grass and cloud and all that can be

named, for we find ourselves struggling
just to keep our eyes open.

Hymn to Hera

O most mis-
represented of goddesses,
always one-sidedly portrayed
as nagging shrew,
possessive wife,
as persecutor of illegit-
imately conceived heroes,
like the humble familial
sphere you jealously protect,
few appreciate your value.
Yours are the harsh vendettas,
but also the tender vows,
the serpent assassins
sent to strangle
baby Herakles in his crib,
but also the blessings
laid upon Jason,
that handsome youth born of
two committed mortals.
Yours are the warm
spaces where families gather,
the kitchens and living and
dining rooms through which
effervescent children, creaking
grandparents, mothers and
fathers and loaves of whole-
hearted bread, precariously
balanced plates heaped with plentiful
mounds of food, strewn toy
building blocks, beloved
dollies and the billowing
smell of thyme and broth and roasted
garlic endlessly circulate.
Yours is the marriage

bed, the sudden flowering
of nature that erupted
upon the occasion
of your sacred union with Zeus.
And yours are the vigilant
eyes in a peacock's
tail, always open,
overseeing. Yours,
the bedtime story. Yours,
the favorite picture
book read aloud a second,
a third and fourth time. Yours,
the miracle of a newborn,
suckling. With gold
wedding bands, with old
photo albums, with house-
hold chores and family movie
nights and have-a-good-day
kisses, you bind us
to each other and
to the precious daily
life we inhabit together.

A House Blessing

Gods bless this house.
Bless it from
the peak of its roof
down to the dark

depths of its foundation.
Bless its brick
walls, built for holding
the outside out,

the inside in,
and also bless
its windows,
its doors,

designed to open
communication
between in-
side and out.

Many rooms,
many inter-
connected chambers form
the heart of our

beloved house.
Bless them all.
Bless each
according to its

given purpose.
Bless the obvious
and privileged
spaces, the family-,

dining- and bed-
rooms where we
gather, converse,
eat, play, make

love and rest. Bless
the kitchen that
offers us its range
upon which to

prepare our food.
Bless the study,
walled with books,
that quiet wing

of knowledge. But
likewise bless
the less celebrated
corners, the bathroom,

basement, attic,
the margins
where we store
our clutter, wash

off or flush
away our dirt,
our waste. Suffused
with light yet

gracious host to
ample pockets
of shadow, a house
must maintain

a delicate balance.
Hold ours in

equilibrium so that
hallways lined

with portraits of
deceased loved
ones might lead us
solemnly into the past,

while at the same
time children's toys
strewn across the
hardwood floor

point toward
our spirited son,
our greatest
hope and future.

Household gods,
bless and also
faithfully in-
habit our house.

Let it stand
like an altar,
like a hallowed cross-
roads where

the visible welcomes
the invisible
and the living
recall the dead.

Junk Totem

The son in the basement
Gleefully breaks through
The shell of a rusted toaster
Hammers out into the nude
Buried inner mechanisms
Sprung-forth springs

A mica plate unscrewed
While his father does
What watchful fathers do
Collects scattered pieces
Salvages the strewn
Guts of a VCR prized open

Doll arms legs toy helicopter
Blades circuit boards like cast-
Off cities of tomorrow
Seen from a bird's-eye view
All these disconnected wonders
Must be playfully inspected

Weighed by child's hand held
Up to light & imbued
With a sense of how scrap
Heaped stripped of context
Longs to reassemble crudely
Displays potential to fuse

Together in one magic beast
The pain of having been
Ripped in two it's always
The son in the basement who
Initiates this transformation
Hops dancing up when sheet

Metal cylinder & dusty
Globe fit neat when inter-
Locking cogwheel
Owl eyes gnash their teeth or
Old mommy shoe makes
Weapon beak it seems

Father has freely granted
His son permission to choose
Son destroyer/creator
Father preserver/protector
Both kneeling down to consecrate
A strange new ancestor

Still Life with Child

Still never holds
Our dining room table
Long enough to paint
An accurate picture

Unless painting
Moves like Soren
All the time in
All directions

All at once a
Vase missing its
Flowers plugged
With three bananas

Spread removed
Become a cape our
Used-to-be bowl of
Fruit now turned

Into a bad decision
Helmet no make
That a sloshing
Pool for Lego

Swimmers each
Crashing navel
Orange jazz
Apple meteor

Splashing water
Water staining
Table's naked
Wood oh well

It's hard to tell
If towered library
Books now toppling
Down to &

Across the floor
Have been saved
From wet or only
Risk alternative

Damage oh well
It's hard to tell
If the missing
Flowers just

Found in the freezer
Were planted there
Meaning to perish
Or preserve them

Suddenly brushes
Appear squeeze-twisted
Tubes of paint &
Soren is painting

The flowers not
Their likeness but
Actual red rose
Petals torn from

Blooms & daubed
Titanium white then
Pressed into paper
Already back-

Grounded thick
With gluey Van

Gogh impasto
Spirals paint

Running down the
Stems of the flowers
Flowers falling into the
Paint cloudy fruit

Bowl of Lego
Water oh well
It's hard to tell
A big mess from

A masterpiece.

An Anything Machine

can only be made
from anything at all
like wadded balls
of masking tape

giveaway plastic
soldiers no one's played with
for at least a thousand
days & warped

boards nailed loosely
together any which way.
Maybe the toy soldiers
are cocooned within

the balls of tape like spider's
prey or project out
on copper wires (wrapped
around their waists)

that secure them to the larger
mother structure
like spacewalking astronauts
like fetuses barking

at the end of taut
umbilical chains.
Maybe the boards
are pocketknife-scored

are splatter-painted pink
& green are drizzle-glued
& dusted with feathers
while a few crude

but recognizable organs
fill the hollow cavity
inside the makeshift
wooden frame: vacuum

hose intestines a broken
treadmill motor heart.
Maybe nature plays a part:
some trailing strands

of ivy or winged
maple seeds a rose
pinched from our neighbor's bush
now stapled to the all-

embracing scheme.
But whatever my son builds
he calls it a machine & his
builds are always spreading

like weeds down in
our basement. As he
widens their sprawling reach,
as he waters them with

hammer blows I listen & dream
of spending the rest of my life
writing a single poem
one that just keeps growing

a poem like a trash heap
a poem like a crackpot machine
a bricolage hodgepodge
contraption poem

about a shoe without a mate
about an empty birdcage

about the pit inside
a sticky Medjool date

about stray dogs
prosthetic limbs & five
deflated volleyballs. A poem
made from anything at all.

Ear Boy & Finger Cat:
Poems for Soren

MYSTERIES OF THE EAR

Little boy did you know
there's another little boy
a boy even more playful
much tinier than you
dwelling down inside
the snail shell of your ear?

He looks just like you except
he's formed of wax and string.
He smells just like you except
he reeks of musty leaves.
He doesn't have a mommy or
a daddy but this is not

a bad thing because . . .
well, because your ear
is filled with slimy
dark canals and because
this would worry a mommy or
a daddy but most of all because

the little boy alive inside
your ear is just too busy
playing with his tools
which are your body's smallest
most delicate-powerful
bones. There's a hammer

buried somewhere in the
middle of your ear and little
ear boy loves to swing it.
There's an anvil and a drum
he pounds on in the darkness
the close heavy dimness

filling the unlit workshop
where his wee shoulders hunch
over his dark designs. Is he
slowly shaping the darkness
around him into a coat
of armor? Or has he been forging

an eensy sword so clever
it can cut through a grownup's
lies? And why does he hold a bone
called the stirrup in his hand
when a stirrup is meant to hold the foot
of a messenger riding a horse?

This tells me there must be
horses at play in your ear. This
tells me someone rides them
rides these dark horses. Someone
carries the little boy's secret
metallic gifts toward you in the night.

FINGER CAT

A Bedtime Story

1

Finger cat lived under seven blankets of toast.
He couldn't borrow a headache. He tried to fly
but his ladder melted a barn of fat policemen.
He tried to swim but his bucket dug a hole
in the ground and disappeared. No one believed him.
They all thought cotton balls were meaner
than one-eyed yellow popsicle sticks. Nose cat sniffled
and elbow cat cried. Ear cat climbed a mountain pickle

and mouth cat sang a song about it.
Then something funny happened one day
because an alarm clock married the color orange.
The color blue forgot its name. Finger cat
loved the color blue. He didn't want to go to sleep.
He wanted to wrestle the bathtub. He didn't want
to visit China. He wanted to smell the moon.
He wanted to bark like a hat and stay awake forever.

2

Finger cat became an orphan chair named
belly button science experiment. He plugged
his junkyard into ten kinds of nonsense.
Arm cat was the bicycle chain and leg cat
smoked the electromagnet. Up cat was the steering wheel
and down cat ate the jumper cables. Their claw
machine was pretty soon and all the stars
in the sky got jealous. Who are finger cat's balloons?

They shaved catapults and whistled until
the only cavemen left for them to play with

invented the word goodnight. Where do the tomorrow
wagons? Finger cat put on his toothbrush.
Then he combed his prayers. Finger cat washed
his lazy homework. Then he kissed his pajamas.
He said he still wanted to stay awake
forever but his bed was too soft to believe him.

THE IMPOSSIBLE PLAYGROUND

A Finger Cat Poem

1

Finger cat and his best liquid possum
wanted to build an impossible playground
to see if their tails might turn to gold
when dipped in an overdue library book.
They stole the wrong flavor of equipment for the job.
Now all they needed were a few empty pockets.

But the sky overhead was already filled
with strange pieces of furniture. The ground
underfoot hid too many dinosaur bones.
And the wind in between said it was busy
sucking mountains through a straw.
(Merry-go-rounds spin nothing but lies…)

They were still looking for a place to unload
their fleas when a lost peanut butter
backpack forgot he wasn't invited. Their playground
woke up from dreaming about haircuts
and flickered like a dying candle sandwich.
A circle could no longer fix anything.

A thank you could no longer harm anyone.
A school bus could jump off the diving board.
Finger cat and the other ingredients
mixed themselves together. Falling
up a jungle gym was the last bag
of sugar left in the neighborhood.

2

Finger cat thought hatching a swing set from an egg
was the same thing as drawing a picture of a nap.
Birdwing thought feathers held faster than screws.
Liquid possum poured himself down the drain.
One by one, their buttery slides collapsed
before a tool could even start building them.

That's when the number 5 came to the rescue.
She'd been to school for one whole day.
She told finger cat, "An impossible
playground is nothing at all like a riddle.
It's more like a nose where children swing directly
from monkeys instead of monkey bars."

CUCKOO HAIKU*

Composed by Finger Cat

1

Feeding socks into a
parking meter beehive.
Normal morning.

2

Letter in the snail-
box today, licking
its slimy grocery bag earrings.

3

Caught a pair of binoculars
spying on my elbow grease.
Breakfast!

4

A microwave rocking horse
popcorn elevator? Never
trust the squirrels.

5

Don't care if
the tulips evaporate. More
trampoline bowling balls please!

6

Nine rabbits, an attic,
the state of Wisconsin: things
I hid in the garden hose.

7

Next time, I'll remember
to grow a pair of wings
before I fly away.

8

Innocence—making
sure no one sees me
when I dip the radio puppet.

9

All you old beards
gone to sleep—
Hello a lot!

10

Lovely weather. Nice to be
outside, dodging
poisonous arrows.

11

Urgent question:
What is this stuff
my fishhook keeps leaking?

12

A face that whistles
like mine is trapped
inside the sticky mirror.

13

Slow motion day.
Sick of watching
newspapers row a boat through the soup.

14

Stole my own tail.
Now I'll never have to learn
how to count to 1!

15

Under my pillow
I hear yellow crayons
wishing they were fuzzy guitars.

16

Puddle of bookshelves
glued to my eyebrows.
Perfect disguise!

*Note to Soren: Haiku is a traditional form of Japanese poetry. A haiku has only three lines and typically consists of a direct observation from nature. (Each line is also supposed to have a fixed number of syllables, but Finger Cat doesn't follow this rule, and neither do many English translators of Japanese haiku.) Here's a famous example written by the Japanese poet, Basho:

Old pond.
A frog jumps in.
Plop!

And here's another example by my favorite writer of haiku, Issa:

New Year's Day—
everything is in blossom!
I feel so-so.

How are Finger Cat's haiku different from Basho's and Issa's? How are they similar? Do you think Finger Cat's haiku would make Basho and Issa laugh?

FINGER CAT'S INVENTION

It looks like a pickled boot.
It looks like a chewed-up helicopter.
It looks like what you get when thirty
    children made from sleeping
        bags blow their noses on the same turtle.
It looks like something
    dumped on the side of the road
        rolled down the length of a hill
    left half-buried in bubbling mud.
It looks like a board game.
It looks like a battlefield.
It looks like someone spliced together
    a trash heap and a toy factory.
It looks like a big mess.
It looks like a small miracle.
    I wouldn't trust it to scratch my back but
it looks like quite a babysitter.

It seems to be made of quicksilver.
It seems to have arms and legs
    three heads and a tail
        a cockpit a swimming
    pool and a passenger seat.
It seems like it would be heavy
    to lift and yet
it only weighs as much as a bowl of dehydrated fleas.
It seems unlikely.
It seems restless.
It can be heard
    puttering around the house at night
        rearranging
    the furniture with a wrecking ball
        repotting the plants
    in quicksand

        making little backfire
    hiccup sounds.

It has a half-
    life of its own.
It tap-dances at funerals
    weeps at birthday parties
        blows its whole paycheck
    on lottery tickets.
It wears a fake mustache
    and makes you feel like a ghost just entered the room
        or like you're a farmer who suddenly threw
    her scarecrows in a bonfire
        and moved away to Thailand.

It comes with a shredded owner's manual.
It leaks mousetraps and cornflakes and motor oil.
It doesn't speak English
    or follow simple directions.
It doesn't pass inspection.
It doesn't care if dirt or grease
    tombstones or Christmas
        trees get under its fingernails.
    Like a hawk with glitter
        and flashlights
    sprinkled all over its body,
it sits on the fence.
It doesn't make sense.
It's not allowed to.

FINGER CAT'S MENAGERIE

Rainbow skunk
Fool's dragon
Vampire dove
Carnivorous lamb

Sewer unicorn
Bearded mermaid
Grizzly hare
Inside-out snake

Dystopian sloth
Loch Ness tadpole
Common sphinx
Buzzard that lays golden eggs

Rottweiler mouse
Feathered monkey
Lava otter
Web-footed angel

III.

Wonder Cabinet

1

Inspired by the Ole Worms
and Johannes Settalas of olde,
my eight-year-old son collects
curiosities from the world
around him and displays them
on a bookshelf in his bedroom.

After my morning coffee,
he and I often stand before
his humble museum,
rock or bird or other field-
guide passing back
and forth between us,

hoping to clearly identify
some cluster of purple
crystals, some darkly
mottled feather, an anonymous
snakeskin peeled wet
from a stone down by the creek.

Sometimes the day's allotted
mystery is easy to solve. "These
must be amethyst crystals formed
over the course of 200 million
years in the womb of a geode." Or,
"This is a wild turkey feather."

Sometimes we discover
we know less than we thought
we knew when the day began.
Maybe a bulbous fossil we once

presumed was the immature
crown of an ancient crinoid,

its feathery arms still folded
up shyly inside a calyx,
needs to be re-envisioned. (We've realized:
A crinoid doesn't flower.
It's an animal, not a plant. So what
is this fossilized sea-bud?*)

Maybe we learn that judging
a serpent by its sloughed-off
skin alone is impossible, but
imagining what type of local
snake might have left a transparent
strip of itself for us to run

through our fingers, using the term
ecdysis, calling a dead crayfish
afloat in a jar of rubbing alcohol
by its Latin binomial name:
these are perfect excuses to contemplate
particular things we love.

2

This past October in Bethlehem,
PA, my son and I drifted
along the boundary of a ruined
steel mill. I was in need
of coffee and a little time
to myself after a week

spent keeping our child
busy while my wife researched
Moravian missionary history.
The afternoon was too windy

and cold. The Museum of
Industry, closed on Mondays.

I snapped at Soren
when he tried to climb
the hurricane fence
for only the second time.
Maybe because a child's
eyes are closer to the ground,

he was the first to notice:
dried yellow wheels of grass
blown up against the chain-link.
Probably just dead weeds,
but to me they evoked crowns
of golden wheat, and I couldn't help

placing one upon each of our heads.
Did the weather really improve
as we more cheerfully picked our way
toward the towering blast furnace,
as we gathered these chance
wreaths in our arms, bestowing

them like blessings on a few
passing strangers? Or had I been
improved, changed by magic
weeds into a clown, a fool
who wears his humors, the foul and
the fair as lightly as straw?

Three days later, I was still picking tiny
seeds out of Soren's long red hair.
Three months later, I can still visit
Soren's cabinet and cup
those seeds, that after-
noon in the palm of my hand.

3

We call the game: *What is it really?*
We like to play in the evening when
Soren's cabinet is dark and shining
a flashlight on nacreous seashells,
polished gemstones, even bleached bones
brings them strangely to life.

Tonight Soren begins with
a pinecone. I say: "It's an egg
laid by a Christmas tree." Courtney says:
"It's a Buddhist temple… for ants."
Soren says: "It's a hand grenade."
Courtney selects some peacock ore.

Soren says: "It's angel poop!"
Courtney says (out of turn): "It isn't
poop! It's an offering to Hera
because her sacred
bird is the peacock." I say: "It's a hunk
a miner chipped off the rainbow."

My choice: a pristine
ammonite fossil. Soren says
(out of turn): "It's a curled up
dragon with its head tucked under
its body. An English wyrm."
Courtney says: "It's a spiral galaxy."

But what is it really? In a
moment of weakness, I take this
question seriously and proclaim:
"It's a whirlpool drawing us
down into the bottomless
depths of reality."

*Our "sea-bud" turned out to be a fossilized blastoid, a prehistoric echinoderm and close relative of the crinoid. In other words—still not a plant!

65

At the Playground

For our friends at the PALS Homeschooling Co-Op

All the kids in my Active Imaginative
Play class insist: They have magical powers.
One little girl tells me she's training
her shadow to fight her enemies.

Twin boys, pulling at each of my shirtsleeves,
want to make sure I know they're invisible,
want me to chase what I cannot see.
And so I commence an elaborate search,

poking my nose under every
bench, kicking every vacant swing,
swiping at the empty air,
while more and more children

disappear, laugh, dodge out of reach.
Then Sadie declares she's a voodoo doll.
She can hurt me by pinching
the skin on her arm. And I play

along—("Ouch!")—swatting
at whatever stung me—("What if
it was a bee? I'm highly allergic!")—
Better check myself into Time Out

Hospital for Grown-Ups.
Doctor's orders: go catch my breath
while sitting under a locust tree.
By now the kids are completely

lost in the stories they're busy
enacting. They're dinosaur-ninja-

princess-zombies, and I bring them here
because children need to feel

such powerful characters are their own.
And yet from my current vantage point,
detached from the game, observer in the shade,
forty years old this coming fall,

having once been a child, a student,
being now a husband, a father, I know
these roles don't belong to the actors. They play
over us like angled sunlight

flickers on silver monkey bar rings,
shine through us as if our hearts were cut
from the same translucent stuff
as the beads on Sadie's friendship bracelet.

And what role am I playing today?
The one where I don't get much of a break
because I hear myself being called
back to chasing invisible children.

After Pythagoras

1

When my son and I study
his favorite subject, Geometry,
or any other branch of mathematics,
what are the full dimensions
of the knowledge to which we aspire?

(The ancient Ionian
philosopher Pythagoras
lived in the 6th century
BCE. He thought the world
derived from numbers,
that the planets, sun,
moon and stars revolved
around the earth in precise
harmonic intervals, emitting
a cosmic symphony only
enlightened souls could hear.
Kepler, Newton, Einstein—all
math-minded modern
scientists belong
to this pure
Pythagorean tradition.)

What secret but orderly
God are we invoking?
What mystical beliefs
are we implicitly asserting
about a right triangle
about a grain of sand
about the entire cosmos
when we say $c^2 = a^2 + b^2$?

(Pythagoras discovered

the five regular solids. To him
and his followers, "the
principles of mathematics
were the principles
of all things."* Some say
his thigh was made of gold.
Pythagorean initiates
were forbidden to eat beans.
No one knows why.)

When we trace a sweeping
arc with the silver
arm of our compass,
when we follow this impulse
the whole way around,
what myth are we drawing
upon? What recurring
Greek dream are we
measuring with
the translucent half-
moon of our protractor?

(A line by definition
extends in both directions forever.
A circle has no beginning.
A circle has no end.
A circle describes the trans-
migration of the soul.)

Is beauty simply
a matter of proportion? Evil,
a form of imbalance?
When we fall in love
do we fall according
to a rhythmic spiral pattern?

(Pythagoras instructed
men as well as women

in the sacred art of numerology.)
Are all of our emotions
songs, serene or raging,
ecstatic or melancholy
ratios plucked on
the strings of a lyre?
(Until the age of forty,
he secluded himself
inside an extinct volcano.)

2

My son and I, drawn close
together at the dining room table,
lean over an open Geometry textbook,
a smeared sheet of graph paper.

The sun is going down,
and our workspace, near a window,
is sharply divided into
planes of light and shadow.

Tonight's lesson carries over
from yesterday and the
day before that. First we deduce
an unknown angle. Then we diagram

the logic. We do the math,
then step outside
to test if perchance,
perhaps, just maybe,

we've attuned our ears
to the music of the spheres.

*From Aristotle's *Metaphysics*

Driving to the Grocery Store

Late February 2020

After listening to five
shocking minutes of NPR,
I switch off the car radio,
try to concentrate instead

on tuning into you,
my passenger, my son,
because I'm worried
that today's particular

edition of bad
news may have
profoundly threatened
your sense of well-being.

We've just heard experts
confirm: A rampaging,
world-conquering virus,
named for its crown,

its blood-red corona
of spikes, will soon
be arriving
in our country,

in our city,
upon our very street,
where, like an invading
army it will lay

waste or at least lengthy
siege to our lives.

Schools will be forced
to close. Stores and

restaurants, libraries
and playgrounds will
empty as hospitals
and graveyards fill. To my own

stunned ears, this big
scary story evokes
the darkest chapters
of the Bible, or maybe

a post-apocalyptic
fable like Cormac
McCarthy's *The Road*.
And in a strange

way, I find these re-
semblances comforting.
Also, my fear is
given contour,

shaped and made partial-
ly graspable by
previous experience,
by difficult but

formative memories:
my brother Andy's
funeral, his embalmed body
displayed like a pale

wax double
of the young man
I loved, or the time
I held a woman

named Carol's hand
as she suffered
through a long
rattling chain of final

breaths. Images
of death: Already
I live among them.
But how is a nine

year-old child—you
who are not even
old enough to ride
securely in the front

seat of our car—
supposed to orient him-
self, his tender
psyche when faced

with impending disaster?
I study you, your neutral
expression in the rearview
mirror. I ask you what

you're thinking and
you're happy to tell me
all about pulley/bucket
systems, pop-up

flags and falling
hammers, board
bouncers, slow
spinners, funnel

and seesaw and zigzag
ramps, each a facet
of the intricate Rube
Goldberg machine

you've been busy
mentally designing
this whole time.
And I realize that,

for you, blessed
child, the future
does not yet signify
loss or risk but only

creative possibilities.
Even as the advancing
enemy's sword prepares to
wound you, even as the

sky smolders weirdly
red in the distance,
for a fleeting
while longer,

a few more car rides,
a few more hours
or days or weeks,
you will remain

untroubled, somehow
shielded by your innocence,
deaf to all prophecies
of doom.

Family Hike: Summer 2020

1

Out here in a protected
woods in Western Pennsylvania,
it almost seems possible
to forget the cruel disease
menacing our species,

the refrigerated trucks
racked full of human corpses,
the deathly silent streets
of all our desperate
locked-down cities. Out here

we can almost believe: At last
we've entered a friendlier
dimension of quiet,
one less haunted, less
tragically wrought

from cold funereal
marble, a living temple
filled with the musical
silence of fiddle-
ferns. Sheltered by leafy

green arches, led
down a wide and well-
blazed trail, having crossed
a few shallow non-
threatening streams,

how quickly we grow secure
enough to slip

off our uncomfortable
masks. And for the first
time in months,

we feel at home, at ease
with the world and
with ourselves, as firmly
rooted as these white
oak and pitch pine

and seven hundred year-
old hemlock trees
in what appears to be
a peaceful natural order.
Held in peace,

we hold our peace.
We have no need
to speak, for all our pleasant
thoughts and feelings
are already spoken, fully

articulated by
ample carpet-
beds of moss, the crisp
fir needles we crush
between our fingers

in order to more deeply
release their fragrant essence. This is
who we think we are, or at least
who we think we once
were and will be

now again forevermore:
the three of us, children,
walking in a forest-
garden, sustained,
together, always.

Until we sense
something gray, uncanny,
sweeping in to perch
up and to the left
at the periphery of our vision.

2

All it takes is an owl—
a barred owl, a night
hunter normally banished
from the light of day.
All it takes is an owl—

voracious, irrepressible
appetites swirling
down in the depths of
its deep-set black eyes.
All it takes is an owl—

the rip and rupture
portended by its keen
beak, its inescapable
talons to challenge
our tender new faith in

nature's designs.
An owl has torn through
the veil separating
the night from the day.
An owl has broken through,

has broken open
the body of our meek
and clumsy quiet
in order to feed
its own stealthy body,

in order to strengthen
its own predatorial silence.
An owl has torn through
our afternoon, has gripped
and then carried us

back to the vulnerable
position from which
we started. Soon we will feel
compelled to speak
of, to discuss and de-

limit this silent owl.
Soon we'll deflect
its ill omen with
a commanding turn of phrase
like "facial disc"

or "rare diurnal appearance."
We will try to flee
into studied speech
just like we tried to
retreat into wild silence.

But for a startled
moment, we can neither
speak nor keep
silent. We can only
gasp, exclaim.

Watching My Son Sleep

1

My child, even as you lie
angelic, seemingly at peace,
I fear that a secret
tide may be gathering
to suddenly crash
against your body,

to seize you in its frothing
arms and shake
your entire being.
Like earlier this summer,
when spiking waves
first flooded your brain.

A rattling bed-
frame, the eerie sound
of your tongue sucking
the back of your teeth
woke your mother
whose cries woke me.

And for those few
eternal minutes that
for me will never
come to an end—
without a second thought,
I prayed over you,

prayed for your safety,
even though I don't believe
in the efficacy
of discursive prayer.

I prayed, and in a way,
my prayers were answered.

A few weeks later,
the neurologist assured us:
only on rare occasions
do children with benign
rolandic epilepsy
die in their sleep.

2

You were somewhere
between the ages of
three and five and probably
don't remember much
of our family trip
to Vancouver Island.

Maybe you've even forgotten
the rugged coastline
of black volcanic rock,
the unequivocal signs
that read "DANGER:
KEEP OFF!" and how

your little hand kept pulling
and pulling at my own
hand which held you back,
even as you begged me
to let you venture forth
and explore the forbidden

pits and crags. But
silently the perilous rocks
called to me as well.
In their massive

stillness they beckoned.
And so, near the end of day

three, you and I
traversed them together.
Not as steep as they appeared
from a distance: more
tiered, ascending and de-
scending in gradual stages,

though your poor mother
later told us that from where
she stood back among
the pine trees her beloveds
seemed to be crawling straight
up and down sheer cliff.

3

Only upon approaching
the very brink, the shifting
and contested border-
line between land and sea,
did I begin to understand why
warning signs had been posted.

(Only upon waking
just now at 3 a.m.—
the hour of your first
seizure—only as I sit watch
over you do I encounter
the full surge of my fear.)

The growling roar. The
hissing spray. No hope for any
child who might happen
to drop down into

the boiling cauldron
crevices between rocks.

(The full risk of loving you
here among the battered
headlands of early
morning: I can worry
myself senseless, blind
even to your sleeping beauty,

but I cannot keep you safe.)
And yet an instinct for self-
preservation seemed to guide you.
You shied well back
from the treacherous
edges, focusing instead

upon the inner tide pools.
For it was never the thrill
of danger but the promise
of life, of slippery and
strange marine organisms
that drew you to this place.

4

Watching you sleep this *matins*,
no longer will I pray
for your safety
because I know that such
petitions always ask too much.
(Nearly luminous

lemon-yellow sea slugs.)
Dangerous are the dream
rocks you presently wander,
searching their pools for living

images to carry back
with you, if only

as memories into the day. (Anemones
that seemed to wave
hello to you in the underwater breeze.)
Let me more simply
let your life be what it is.
Let respect but never fear

of death be your life's limit. (Razor-
encrusted barnacles. Purplish
pin-cushion urchins.
And the singular
treasure you longed to
chance upon most of all:

a tubular-
footed sea star
suctioning itself vertically
to an algae-slick
submerged stone
surface.)

Let me
let your feet
take their own
sure-enough hold.
Let me
let go.

Dear Soren (Ode to a Geode)

Summer 2021

Well, it's been one
hell of a year,
and we haven't been
back here, back home
to Jasper, Indiana,
the town where I
grew up, the town
where your beloved
Grandma Marsha lives,
since the first summer
of the pandemic.
It's been roughly
a year since we last
walked past the hill-
side cemetery where
your Uncle Andy
is buried, since we
last stopped to place
a jar of dill pickles
upon his grave, then
carried on without him
a few more blocks
down Bartley Street,
eventually arriving
at what used to be
called the Providence
Home for Retarded
Men (did they ever bother
to rename it something
more politically
correct?) and the geode
grotto that graces

its open public
grounds. You ask
me to bring you here
every time our
family visits Jasper.
And so we're
here now, once again,
the same two
people visiting
the same familiar
place. Except that,
in the past year, the entire
world and everyone
in it has changed.
Uncharacteristically
hesitant to climb
the niched and bumpy
geode-studded walls,
the honeycomb
cement work
embedded with
little trinkets, green,
blue and rose-
colored shards of glass,
turquoise bracelet
beads, pennies, creamy
pink-lipped seashells,
cautiously testing
each foothold,
going only so far
before pausing
to ask for your father's
help, you are no longer
the fearless little
boy who once
upset his mother
when he claimed
he could survive being

run over by a speeding
car. And not merely
survive it, but even
rise up and walk
away. Unscathed.
(This invincible
attitude first changed
late last spring,
the night you burst
weeping through
our bedroom door, sob-
scared of COVID,
needing to retreat, at least
for a tender while,
back into the nest-
like, the parent-
packed safety of
co-sleeping.)
As for me,
I feel as if I've
aged a decade
in a single year,
as if a relentless
angel had pressed
my face too long,
too close to a
desiccating
flame of worry.
The lockdown
and just after
that another
victim of racist
law enforcement,
George Floyd,
murdered by police
right out in the open,
right out in the middle
of a Minneapolis

street. Your mysterious
seizures and climate
change—in the
news for weeks,
infernal visions
of the California
skies, choked with
smoke, with wild-
fire and brimstone.
(Keep America
Great!) Your mother's
fall, her fractured
spine, preceded
by the bitterly
contested election,
the capitol riots,
our country's right-
wing still flapping
in the dust, still
hoping to stir up
conspiracy whirl-
winds where there
are no substantial
grains of evidence
to support their lies.
But haven't we all
been lying to our-
selves and each
other for so
long that none of
us exactly
qualifies as
scrupulous?
For my part,
I've been less than
honest concerning
my (previously latent)
vanity. I used to

claim I didn't
give a shit about
mere appearances.
Now every time
I encounter
my aging, my care-
worn, my deep-
lined, my large-
pored, my slack-
skinned, my eye-
bagged, my sun-
spotted face
in the bathroom
mirror, I'm
haunted by
an image of
myself I barely
recognize. Who
is this withered,
weather-beaten
stranger? And more
importantly, what
have I become
that I find this
stranger's marked
but harmless visage
so threatening?
All year long,
I guess we've all
been delivered unto
the unwelcome
process of losing
certain things,
things we inevitably
took for granted,
things we knew
were never really
ours to keep, even though

it once was easy
to go on pretending
otherwise. Our
youth, our health,
our homes, our lives,
our loved ones,
our minds or
maybe just our faith
in ourselves or in
our democracy. This
year we all lost
something irreplaceable.
But as I watch
you finally give up
your efforts to sur-
mount the tallest
of the grotto's
roofless outer
walls, as I stand
beneath you,
spotting you
on your return
to the ground
where I gather you
into a hug, never fully
releasing my embrace,
leaving my right arm
draped across your ever-
broadening shoulders
the whole time we
circle back around
to the cave-like inner
entrance, progressing
slowly past the
stations of the cross,
I begin to tell you
the story of the Italian
immigrant who

built this un-
heralded folk-art
shrine. By the time
he was your age,
Father Phillip
Ottavi had already
suffered more than
you and I combined
have yet to or
may ever suffer.
He lost his entire
family in the catastrophic
Messina earthquake
of 1908, was raised
in an orphanage
run by Saint Luigi
Orione and eventually
came to Jasper
in order to serve
the disabled men
at the Providence
Home. And yet,
even as he aspired to
live by his Savior's
gentlest teaching—care
for the meek,
for the sick
and unfortunate —
an unyielding grudge
prevented him from
loving the humblest,
most simple of all
created things—
rocks and pebbles,
the very stones
of which
God's earth is
composed. Every

night in his
dreams, he re-
lived the betrayal.
Stone structures,
trusted to hold,
to support his city,
his precious child-
hood, his family,
suddenly trembling
like weak flesh, then
failing altogether,
sealing him
within a dark
and evil womb
of rubble. (How many
timeless hours
did his litho-
thropy gestate
before rescuers
finally bore him,
parentless,
from the total
ruins?) And every
day, every time
he attended mass—
St. Joseph's Church,
its brown sand-
stone blocks hewn
and ferried all
the way from Europe,
his distant home-
land, as if God
Himself refused
to let Father Phillip
forget the hard-
ship that had formed him
and would always
define him. The mild

priest longed to kick
those smug bricks.
I believe it was
Paracelsus, the great
alchemist-physician,
who said *similia
similibus curantur*
("like cures like").
In the case of
Father Phillip,
stones themselves—geodes—
healed the earlier
wounds inflicted
by some of their less
compassionate
fellows. Dull, pitted,
lumpy and lop-
sided on the
surface, the humble
geode houses
an interior treasure—
milk white,
moon yellow,
royal purple
crystals, each
glittering
concretion pre-
cipitated secretly,
patiently over
many millions
of years. First
stumbling upon these
awkward egg-like
rocks, first learning
of their hidden
riches when he sought
a plentiful local
material with which

to build the Holy
Mother a grotto
modeled in spirit
upon the one
in Lourdes, Father
Phillip soon
realized his visionary
project would be
more than just
a devotional
offering. Over-
seeing the daily
work, helping to
unload the crates
of geodes dredged
muddy from
a creek-bed up
in Heltonville,
learning to properly
handle the stones,
to wash them
and then care-
fully crack
a chosen few
open became a
personal healing
process, a way
to practice not
only accepting
but even searching
out and admiring
the divine
beauty and purpose
concealed within
all things, especially
one's seeming
enemies. It took ten
years, a round

decade (1960-1970),
to complete both
the geode grotto and
Father Phillip's
inner trans-
formation. Near
the end of his long
life, at last
he was able to
stand before the finished
marble altar,
before the dark
vault, softly
lit by prayer
candles, by flickering
pockets of crystal
laid into the damp
and cavernous
grotto walls,
before the arching
fountains and
chalice-shaped
birdbaths,
the hopping
robins, darting
sparrows,
the shifty but
lingering crows,
before the
immaculately
pruned rose-
bushes, a stray
patch of dandelions,
able to stand,
free and finally
full of love,
before the entire
breadth and

height and
depth of God's
creation, much
like his patroness
the Virgin
Mary now stood
placidly upon
her pedestal—She
whose concern
for suffering beings
surpasses all
conditions; She
whom he now believed
had wept beside him
there in his pit
of rubble, pitying
him the loss
of his birth parents,
protecting him
from that time
forth and guiding him
gently, in the subtle
and unobtrusive
way that only
a wise and loving
parent can,
toward the
realization of
absolute
peace. Soren:
It's been one
hell of a year,
but here we are,
standing together
in the same deep
sanctuary where
Father Phillip
once stood. You

ask to light a candle,
suddenly rejoice
with your whole
body and spirit
as you choose
the perfect taper
stick, use it
to transfer a fragile
flame from one
candle unto
another, and
in the process,
pass the glow of
your rekindled
child joy
along to me,
your father who
delights in nothing
more than you,
my resilient,
my radiant
son. And while,
as your father,
I'd like to believe
it was my own
parental love
and wisdom that
led us to this brief
reprieve, this dim
reflection of
Father Phillip's
more fully realized
peace, I know,
spiritually,
you and I are
both still children,
shepherded by
an invisible

parent, She
or He who cannot
or will not prohibit
our suffering but
comforts us
with meaning-
laden stones.
Hear their secret
promise: Beneath
our scarred outer
surface, slowly
we are generating
unseen splendor.